50 Testimonial Christian Poems

Light
of the
World

Light of the World: 50 Testimonial Christian Poems...

Nomutsa Oliver Madamombe

Scripture quotations marked (NIV) are taken from the HOLY BIBLE, NEW INTERNATIONAL VERSION® NIV® Copyright© 1973, 1978, 1984, by International Bible Society. Used by permission of Zondervan. All rights reserved.
Scripture quotations marked (KJV) are taken from the Authorized King James version of the Holy Bible.

ISBN: 978-0-7974-8114-5
Published by: Red Rose Poems
Cover Image: Pixabay
Cover Design: Edlight Simeone Maguvu

Acknowledgements

Many thanks to Mutsa & Mai Mutsa, friends and family, Beacon of Hope Fellowship Cape Town, South Africa and Forward in Faith International Ministries Abu Dhabi, UAE. Your love is amazing. May God richly bless you all. Thank you.

Follow on social media:

https://www.facebook.com/nomutsa/

https://www.facebook.com/redrosepoems/

Email: oliver@redrosepoems.com

For

Bethany

Contents

Foreword

Growing up as a young boy I used to distribute the good news of Jesus Christ via The Trumpet of Truth Christian magazines. I could receive loads of these books every month then spread them in my neighborhood as well as at school.

However, there was one simple poem I read and loved so much and it never went out of my head because it inspired me a lot. Probably, it is the reason why I, myself am an author today. Here it is:

I am only one, but still I am one
I cannot do everything but still I can do something
And because I cannot do everything
I will not refuse to do something that I can do

Author unknown

The World's Greatest

Enough is enough!!!
I've gone through all the rough
I am taking territory
I am geared for victory
Don't ask me how
Because my time is now!
I'm more than a conqueror
I shall not be a labourer
When I got sanctified
Truly, I got satisfied
Satan you better flee
I won't tolerate your plea
Now we shall all see
Who shall be driven into the sea
You say you are dreadful?
I say I'm powerful
By now you must be furious
And I'm also serious!
I am waging war
And you are going to fall
Even when you draw near
I will not fear
When you come in like a flood
I'll be covered by the blood
When you try to kill
My Lord will heal
Because in me is the greatest
Jesus Christ, my dearest
Who can suppress it?
When I can confess it

Who can deny it?
When I can define it
Jesus is my Lord
His father is my God
When I preach to all men
They all say amen!

Scripture

And this is the confidence that we have in him, that, if we ask any thing according to his will, he heareth us: And if we know that he hear us, whatsoever we ask, we know that we have the petitions that we desired of him. (1 John 5:14-15 KJV)

He's Alive

From the manger,
To the anger,
He's not real,
He's full of zeal,
Smack Him, smash Him,
Why not save yourself?
Nail Him, spike Him,
Why not call your Lord?
Stone Him, smite Him,
Whose king is he?
Crucify Him, kill Him,
Together with the robbers!
Let him thirsty,
And give Him vinegar,
Let Him suffer and groan,
Groan, groan, groan,
Let Him suffer and die,
Die, die, die,
My father, my father,
This cup, oh father,
Your will be done,
Tears, tears, tears,
Women cried, a distance
But forgive them, oh father,
The body died,
The sun was angered,
The earth was shaken,
He was buried,
Third day, a miracle,
In the grave, was no one,

He went to Heaven,
He sent the Spirit,
He's alive,
Alive, alive, alive

Scripture

For I know [that] my redeemer liveth, and [that] he shall stand at the latter [day] upon the earth: (Job 19:25 KJV)

In His Presence

The Lord made that day,
Behold, it was fine,
The sun cheerfully looked down,
With such a unique and gentle shine,
Sitting and walking in this garden,
Truly reminded me of Eden,

Being showered with blessings,
Naturally fascinating surroundings,
An environment so peaceful,
An atmosphere so conducive,
Appreciating every second of life,
A life of fruitful prophecy,

Living in the garden,
Is living in the presence,
Of the Almighty God,
Who created heaven and earth,
Leaving the garden is,
Leaving the presence of God,

In His awesome presence,
There is manifestation of His essence,
Everything becomes of substance,
But in His absence,
Your well-being is not in balance,
The devil can take a chance!

Scripture

And they heard the voice of the LORD God walking in the garden in the cool of the day: and Adam and his wife hid themselves from the presence of the LORD God amongst the trees of the garden. And the LORD God called unto Adam, and said unto him, Where art thou? (Genesis 3:8-9 KJV)

Truly from Above

My mentor,
You are the master,
What is it that I can learn?
If I cannot learn from you,
The art of doing,
And the doing of art,
Is all housed in you,

My King,
You are the conqueror,
Who is he that can knock me,
When you are by my side,
Not fighting any fights,
But fighting only a good fight,
Against evil principalities,

My God,
You are gracious,
Why can I not love you?
When you'd loved me first,
You sent your only and dearest son,
To die on the cross for me,
His blood washed away my sins,

My blessed Lord,
You are unbeatable,
Nailed on Calvary to die,
But died only to live again,
Oh, what a wonder you are,
The earth shook to acknowledge,

That you are truly from above!

Scripture

And when the centurion, which stood over against him, saw that he so cried out, and gave up the ghost, he said, Truly this man was the Son of God. (Mark 15:39 KJV)

Only in Him

Only in Him,
Is there life,
And by Him,
We do live,
For He is in us all,
And we are all in Him,
Thus, we all live not, but Him

Only in Him,
Is there salvation,
And by Him,
All burdens are carried,
For He died on the cross,
And so did us all with Him,
Thus, we be resurrected to Heaven as Him

Only in Him,
Is there love,
And by Him,
We are commanded to love,
For He had loved us first,
And we love Him as He love us,
Thus, we love our neighbour as we love ourselves

Only in Him,
Is there joy,
And by Him,
All are made joyful,
For Him we sing, praise and worship,
And we give Him all honour and glory,

Thus, we are strengthened because of His joy,

Only in Him,
Is there a way,
And by Him,
Is the only way to the Father;
For He showed us the way,
The truth and the life,
And we believeth in this gospel,
Thus, He will take and lead us to the Father;

Scripture

For God so loved the world, that he gave his only begotten Son, that whosoever believeth in him should not perish, but have everlasting life. (John 3:16 KJV)

Abba Father

To the owner and creator
Of the universe,
Your architecture is next to none,
Your touch is the best
I had ever known,
How unprecedented is
The humanity of mankind,
And the habitation
Of creatures in the forests,
Dwelling together on earth,
To compliment your greatness,
How then,
Could there be another one?
But you Almighty,

Indeed, you are Abba Father,
A Father full of love,
Your one and only begotten son,
You sent to us,
To be slaughtered on the cross,
As a living sacrifice,
To redeem every believer,
From the grip of the devil,
To break lose every chain of Hades,
And in Heaven, on your right
Your beloved son ascended,
How then,
Could there be another one?
But you Almighty,

In the Heaven above
Or down on this earth
Neither in water under the earth,
Is there anyone like you;
We can search for all eternity long,
But still, there is none!
The devil trembles,
At the sound of your name.
And every demon flees,
In your mighty presence,
For you are Holy and righteous,
How then,
Could there be another one?
But you Almighty,

Let them in darkness,
Come to know you Father,
Let your tender mercies,
Befall unto them and give them light,
Let them get knowledge,
To understand your will,
For they are lost!
Wisdom is only for those,
With fear of your greatness,
And eternal life, at no cost
Is the reward for faith in Christ;
How then,
Could there be another one?
But you Almighty.

Scripture: I am the LORD thy God, which have brought thee out
of the land of Egypt, out of the house of bondage. Thou shalt have
no other gods before me. (Exodus 20 v 2-3 KJV)

Be Thankful

The science of breathing,
And the functionality of the body,
As priceless as it is,
How can I be unthankful?

The feel of the nature,
And the creative art of the world,
As beautiful as it is,
How can I be unthankful?

The coming out of the sun,
And the shining of stars by the night,
As miraculous as it is,
How can I be unthankful?

The stretching of the oceans,
And the living of creatures within,
As magnificent as it is,
How can I be unthankful?

The power of the human mind,
And all the advancement in this world,
As innovative as it is,
How can I be unthankful?

The flow of the Holy Spirit,
And all the divine works in this world
As a blessing as it is,
How can I be unthankful?

Thank you once more, Lord Jesus.

Scripture

And whatsoever ye do in word or deed, [do] all in the name of the Lord Jesus, giving thanks to God and the Father by him. (Colossians 3: 17 KJV)

Is It True Lord?

Is it true Lord,
Is it true?
That you created me,
So wonderfully and so fearfully,
Nobody else is like me,

Is it true?
That you loved me first,
When I was lost and in darkness,
You revealed yourself unto me,

Is it true?
That you are mindful of me,
You hear me each time I call,
I'm amazed by your presence,

Is it true?
That you are merciful to me,
When I repent and ask for forgiveness,
You cleanse me and make me pure,

Is it true?
That your love is great,
Deeper than the oceans,
Higher than any mountain,

Is it true?
That you sent your son Jesus,
To die for me on the cross,
I'm rightfully your child oh God,

Is it true?
That you defeated death,
You raised Him on the third day,
And took Him to where you are,

Is it true?
That you want me to dwell in Heaven too,
In your Kingdom of Holiness,
For everlasting, to reign with you
Is it true Lord,
Is it true?

Scripture

Howbeit when he, the Spirit of truth, is come, he will guide you into all truth: for he shall not speak of himself; but whatsoever he shall hear, [that] shall he speak: and he will shew you things to come. (John 16:13 KJV)

My Father

My unforgettable,
My favourite,
My father,
How can I forget you?
How can I not favour you?
When you are my one,
My one and only father,
You raised me up perfectly, father
Through thick and thin,
In the riches and poverty,
You never gave up on me,
You gave me all your love,
You moulded my future,
Like father like son,
So I grew, in your statutes
Forever your teachings are in me,
I'll never forsake you, father
Your presence gives me a feeling,
That feeling of genuine comfort,
Comforting me from all sorrows,
The sorrows and grief of this world,
This world which is incomplete
Incomplete without you, father
You will forever remain,
My unforgettable,
My favourite,
My father.

Scripture: Children's children [are] the crown of old men; and the glory of children [are] their fathers. (Proverbs 17:6 KJV)

The Good Shepherd

I shall forever delight
In Christ Jesus my Saviour
For all He did and all to come
I shall serve no other master but Him
A true and obedient servant, I shall be
With Him, I shall fear no evil
I am more than a conqueror!
No mountain is too big
For me to ever move
No weapon formed against me
Shall ever prosper
Though enemies might flood me
His Spirit will raise a standard
His rod and His staff
Shall forever comfort me
I lift up my soul with trust
I lift up my hands
To glorify His name
My Lord is gracious
He is full of amazing love
He listens to my words in prayer
He is so merciful, He forgives me
My head is raised high by Him
My heart and soul honour Him
He makes me the head not the tail
His blessings flow and overtake me
Exceedingly abundantly above all
I am not cursed, no!
I am forever blessed
He anoints my head with oil

Indeed, He is my shepherd

Scripture

The LORD [is] my shepherd; I shall not want. He maketh me to lie down in green pastures: he leadeth me beside the still waters. (Psalms 23: 1 – 2 KJV)

Christmas Again

On decorated tables
We all dine
Pieces of cakes
And some wine
The family had gathered
It is a time to shine
A smile on every face
Tells everything is fine
Christmas time again
Oh yes, here it is
That time of the year,
Let every nation celebrate
Celebrate the birth of a son
A son gifted to the world
From Heavenly places
To save this world
Which came short of glory
Because of the sinful nature
Since the days of Eve
But this Christmas eve
Let us all reason and
Celebrate with knowledge
Not only is it about eating
It is all about giving
It is all about Jesus!

Scripture

*For God sent not his Son into the world to condemn the world;
but that the world through him might be saved. (John 3: 17 KJV)*

Happy Birthday

To exhale,
To inhale,
To exhale,
To inhale again,
Indeed, it's a gain,
Not by the brain,
Not even in vain,
Comes with no pain,
Like a drop of rain,
Beloved my brethren,
This day you were born,
Many years have gone,
Still you're alive and strong,
Thank God with a song,
For this day is your day,
Not yesterday but today,
Happy birthday, today
Now shall I truly say,
Many years be your way,
Like that I shall pray,
Your cake is in the tray,
More presents on the way,
Enjoy this day!!!

Scripture

Honour thy father and thy mother, as the LORD thy God hath commanded thee; that thy days may be prolonged, and that it may go well with thee, in the land which the LORD thy God giveth thee. (Deuteronomy 5:16 KJV)

Raindrops

Some care less,
But others give full cognisance,
Noting every cloud's movement,
In awe anticipation,
As they become darker and darker,
Up in the sky above,
All lost hope is rejuvenated once more,
For the most precious gift is at hand;
Like a bereaved widow,
Are the darkened clouds,
Making the daylight surrender,
Battle with no choice,
Trying to hold back tears,
But her emotions are running high!
The strong winds came,
Tried to cool things down,
But all in vain,
For the most precious gift is at hand;

Suddenly,
All battle lines are drawn,
No more compromise,
The tears are released,
In tens and dozens even thousands,
It is a race they enjoy,
To see who kiss the ground first,
They all miss the feel of earth,
The dams and the oceans,
For the most precious gift is to become;

Your guess is good;
There is more joy and tribulation,
In all plants and creatures,
Greater and smaller,
Even the earth is smiling,
As she hugs this gift,
All the desire and the waiting,
The hunger and the thirst is gone,
For the most precious gift is here;

Another guess?
Perfect, the presenter deserves a big praise,
The buried seeds now have,
A chance to see the world,
All the fish in seas are geared,
For the long trip to the ocean,
And the farmer is grinning;
He knows harvest shall be a bumper,
For the most precious gift is here!

Scripture

He watereth the hills from his chambers: the earth is satisfied with the fruit of thy works. He causeth the grass to grow for the cattle, and herb for the service of man: that he may bring forth food out of the earth; (Psalms 104: 13 – 14 KJV)

Whole Night Through

I truly missed you,
Whole night through,
My heart went blue,
As I longed for you,

I did not finish,
What I wanted to accomplish,
Yet you left me,
Crying terribly for you,

I'm not happy without you,
My night is long without you,
I feel cold in your absence,
Because you are of substance,

I shall hold on to my hope,
I no longer shall mourn,
My joy will come in the morning,
When you arrive and embrace me,

You bring light in my world,
You make each day meaningful,
Your name is sunshine,
I love you dearly.

Scripture

Jesus answered, Are there not twelve hours in the day? If any man walk in the day, he stumbleth not, because he seeth the light of this world. But if a man walk in the night, he stumbleth, because there is no light in him. (John 11:9-10 KJV)

I am come a light into the world, that whosoever believeth on me should not abide in darkness. (John 12:46 KJV)

The Sun, My Son

Be wise, my son,
Oh be wise,
Let your eyes my son,
Be in your head,
Let no proverb pass,
Without you understanding,
For with it,
Comes all the knowledge,
And the excellence of knowledge,
Is life to those with wisdom,

Be wise my son,
Oh keep my word,
For few are days of a man,
Born of a woman,
Receive my sayings,
And many shall be,
The days of your life,
Stay simple and keep this simplicity,
Happiness will surely follow you,

Be wise my son,
Oh take heed of the sun,
For it rises up every morning,
And gives light to the world,
Likewise, must you rise,
And let your talent shine,
The world is a big stage,
For every one of us,
And indeed it is,

Take the opportunity,

Be wise my son,
Oh make every second count,
The time is ticking,
Stop dreaming in broad daylight,
Make hay whilst sun shines,
Despise procrastination!
For you shall say tomorrow,
Even when tomorrow comes,
And at the end of the day,
Nothing is accomplished!

Be wise my son,
Oh do not worry,
For the rest of your day,
When you stumble and fall down,
Be like the sun, my son, it does fall,
But rises again in the morning,
Never let your dreams crumble,
Because of your downfalls,
And you shall fulfil all your goals
Just like the sun, my son.

Scripture

The fear of the LORD [is] the beginning of wisdom: a good understanding have all they that do [his commandments:] his praise endureth for ever. (Psalms 111:10 KJV)

The Voice of Reason

For trying times are near,
Resentment and ignorance
Both shall bring fear,
Listen to the voice of reason,
It shall remain true in every season,
Why throw yourself in the ocean?
When you cannot swim to the shore!
Why jump off the mountain?
Without any wings on you!
Costly, is every second of bad decision,
Why do you fake it to make it?
Don't you know that,
You have to work it to get it?
Even faith without works is dead!
For with work comes all harvest,
And a good work,
Brings forth a good harvest,
Never allow your mind to be lazy!
For an idle mind,
Is the devil's workshop,
Go to the ant you sluggard!
Consider her ways and be wise,
Are you then anything less than an ant?
Why take fire and put it in your bosom?
No doubt, eventually you'll get burnt!
Why do you put yourself then?
In the company of bad people?
Have you not heard yet?
They corrupt a good mind!
Listen to the voice of reason,

This is your season!

Scripture

The mouth of the righteous speaketh wisdom, and his tongue talketh of judgment. The law of his God [is] in his heart; none of his steps shall slide. (Psalm 37:30-31KJV)

My Inner Me

You me,
My inner me,
You are not my enemy,
Why don't you motivate me?
Give me that power to move on,
That Spirit of overcoming,
Urge me on to fight fear,
The fear which is always haunting me,
Do it now,
My inner me,
My victory shall be your victory too,

You me,
My inner me,
You are not my enemy,
Why don't you encourage me?
I need that positive inspiration from you,
To be my source of strength every time,
That I might not fall short of power,
Whenever the enemy comes against me,
Do it now,
My inner me,
My downfall shall be your downfall too,

You me,
My inner me,
You are not my enemy,
Why don't you support me?
I need your backing when fighting war,
I want to lean on you and trust in you,

After all you know me better than anybody else,
Provide for me, all the necessities,
Do it now,
My inner me,
My success shall be your success too,

You me,
My inner me,
You are not my enemy,
Why don't you love me?
You know most my inner feelings,
Who shall satisfy me, if not you?
Teach me to be patient and to be kind,
Teach me never to fail, please
Do it now,
My inner me,
My happiness shall be your happiness too,

Scripture

Speaking to yourselves in psalms and hymns and spiritual songs, singing and making melody in your heart to the Lord; Giving thanks always for all things unto God and the Father in the name of our Lord Jesus Christ; (Ephesians 5:19-20 KJV)

That he would grant you, according to the riches of his glory, to be strengthened with might by his Spirit in the inner man; (Ephesians 3:16 KJV)

That Spirit

Why search for words,
When your Spirit define better?
Invisible and immeasurable it is,
Yet, very natural too,
No word can define best,
Than feelings do,
Neither is there a phrase,
That gives a better explanation

By a strong passion,
A feeling is patiently created,
And with all sincerity and kindness,
It is fortified,
The desire to attain,
Then drives up the conscience,
The conscience that grips
And controls the mind,
And appropriately, responds the body

When no food tastes good,
Disturbed is the feeling,
And when no sleep comes at night,
Troubled it is,
All is never well with you,
Until the moment the feeling rests in peace,
And this peace,
Is your peace of mind;

I've always wondered how,
You are always simple,

And not boastful,
Persevering and never losing hope,
Rejoicing in truth and never delighting in evil,
But now I know what drives you,
It's that good Spirit in you!

Scripture

But the fruit of the Spirit is love, joy, peace, longsuffering, gentleness, goodness, faith, Meekness, temperance: against such there is no law. (Galatians 5: 22 – 23 KJV)

Love Song

My one and only love
Let me sing
My song to you, with honour
I had sharpened my voice
For this moment
I've been waiting for this day all along
The lyrics and all the sweet melodies
I've collected
And have carefully blended them
Together especially for you
That you might understand
How important you are to me
That you might know
The depth of my feelings
That you get the vision of my expressions
That you see the picture I'm painting
Oh, how I love to admire
Your beautiful structure
My darling, my dove, my dear
My one and only living desire
A rare species!
One of your own kind
How lovely is that shape of you!
Your white teeth
Gives your lovely lips that edge
The edge no other girl has
My queen, you are unique
Your face is ever shining
Your nose was perfectly fitted
With superb craftsmanship

Those firm breasts on your chest
Oh, what a force of attraction!
How peculiar is your voice, honey
Every word that comes
Out of your mouth is magic
You move with such confidence
Miss independent!
Your beauty never cease to amaze me
There is something new
In you every day, my love
I wish I could sing
My song to you forever
But as you are looking back at me
I'm rendered speechless!

Scripture

How beautiful are thy feet with shoes, O prince's daughter! the joints of thy thighs [are] like jewels, the work of the hands of a cunning workman. Thy two breasts [are] like two young roes [that are] twins. (Song of Songs 7: 1; 3 KJV)

This Woman

This woman,
Man's God made partner,
Fearfully and wonderfully created,
From the right hand rib,
Naturally treasured and adored,
She enhances status,
With her you get all respect,
What could be of this world?
If there wasn't any woman,
She's God's love in action,
Her love lasts a lifetime,

This woman,
She heals with her touch,
And her voice consoles,
Her embrace gives life,
In her eyes lies the future,
Her words are meaningful,
And superb is her advice,
Her heart is filled with passion,
And her soul is full of joy,
There is hope in what she believes,

This woman,
She dresses herself with honour,
Her looks are beautiful,
Blessed is her life,
For she also brings life,
God's favour is upon her,
God's Spirit is within her,

Blessed is the man,
Who cherishes this woman,

Scripture

Favour [is] deceitful, and beauty [is] vain: [but] a woman [that] feareth the LORD, she shall be praised. Whoso findeth a wife findeth a good thing, and obtaineth favour of the LORD. (Proverbs 31:30; 18:22 KJV)

My True Rib

You 'happy smiler',
The most adorable one,
Like sunshine,
You brought light in my life,
You are truly my rib,
Most gorgeous,
No word or phrase on earth
Can express how I feel,
My heart leaps with joy
Every time I see you.

You are an original,
A full pack of beauty,
Intact, top, mid and bottom,
All rights reserved!
You can heal any jealous man
From his weakness,
Your force of attraction,
Is an irresistible temptation!
Every dream of you
Is as good as real,

Your touch is unique,
I guess it reverses,
The blood circulation,
Indeed, and a whole lot
Of other biological chemistries!
You took my whole heart,
Can't afford to lose you now,
When you dump me,

Not only is it heartbreak,
But a life-ache as well,

And if I die,
Your beauty might still resurrect me!
Oh, how I love the way you talk,
Or is it the sound of your voice,
The way you say my name,
It sounds unique every time,
The way you walk,
Is just a marvel in its own right;
No wonder why some often say,
'After you, lady'
Can't really express it,
You are just my true rib,

Your smile can kill,
Kindly do it cautiously, I beg
That look in your eyes,
Is gently piercing my soul!
Please do not hug me today;
I guess I need a breast plate first!
My brains are really becoming numb,
'What's my name?'
I'm lost in a new world!
Wait a second…

Scripture

*And the rib, which the LORD God had taken from man, made he
a woman, and brought her unto the man (Genesis 2: 22 KJV)*

Let thy fountain be blessed: and rejoice with the wife of thy youth. [Let her be as] the loving hind and pleasant roe; let her breasts satisfy thee at all times; and be thou ravished always with her love. (Proverbs 5: 18 – 19 KJV)

Promiscuous Girl

She puts on the most expensive,
The dress to entice,
Consciously, she reveals her body
The move to seduce,
Be on guard young man!
For your days she will reduce,
Her lips drip milk and honey,
And her speech is smooth,
But please refuse,
Do a Joseph and run!
Her kiss is very sweet,
And her embrace so warm,
But only to amuse,
No matter how seriously,
You want to settle with her,
She dislikes settling down,
Every drug known and unknown,
She had already used,
But only to abuse!
Young man beware, again I plead
For your feelings she'll arouse,

Promiscuous girl,
Your feet are heading to death!
It's ridiculous,
You lead straight to the grave,
But you can't realise!
Perilous times are nigh,
And verily, you shall regret
In privacy you do maneuver,

Because indeed it is a shame,
Even to your very self!
Being known to every demon,
Queen of the dark emperor, you are
But hear me, I tell you
Be serious girl,
Take this word for a thought,
Gorgeous among nations,
But well respected too,
Don't you desire that?
Promiscuous girl,
REPENT now!
And be transformed,
Better become a precious girl,
Your time is now,
Jesus Christ is knocking;

Scripture

Flee fornication. Every sin that a man doeth is without the body; but he that committeth fornication sinneth against his own body. What? know ye not that your body is the temple of the Holy Ghost [which is] in you, which ye have of God, and ye are not your own? For ye are bought with a price: therefore glorify God in your body, and in your spirit, which are God's. (1 Corinthians 6: 18 – 19 KJV)

The Heartbreak

But why my love, why?
After all the time,
We had shared together,
What about the promises,
That you've made,
Please my love,
Come back to your senses,
What is it that got into you?
That turned your heart into a stone,
The heart I had known,
To be full of love,
Full of patience and full of forgiveness,
I truly can't believe this is happening,
Surely, I bet it's a dream,
I shall work up.

My heart is in great pain, love
The greatest pain I had ever known,
Will I ever be able to love again?
A heart once broken,
Is surely a heart no more!
I can't swallow anything,
And my usual sleep is gone,
I wish I had never known,
Anything called YOU!
From being my dearest,
You are the most horrible,
But why my love, why?
I truly can't believe this is happening,
Surely, I bet it's a dream,

I shall work up!

Scripture

Therefore what God has joined together, let no one separate. When they were in the house again, the disciples asked Jesus about this. He answered, "Anyone who divorces his wife and marries another woman commits adultery against her. And if she divorces her husband and marries another man, she commits adultery. (Mark 10: 9-12 NIV)

Let the morning bring me word of your unfailing love, for I have put my trust in you. Show me the way I should go, for to you I lift my soul. (Psalms 143: 3 NIV)

I'm Sorry

I am sorry,
For all things that I'd said,
And the debts I'd not paid,
All the pain I'd caused,
In your road that I'd crossed,
Please find it in your heart,
To forgive me,

I am sorry,
For all my promises that were lies,
It's a pity that you never realise,
But all this I did scrutinise,
The reason why I want to be nice,
Please find it in your heart,
To forgive me,

I am sorry,
For letting you down my friend,
Maybe it's because I did pretend,
My wrongs are too much to amend,
My road had finally come to an end,
Please find it in your heart,
To forgive me,

Scripture

Be ye angry, and sin not: let not the sun go down upon your wrath: And be ye kind one to another, tenderhearted, forgiving one another, even as God for Christ's sake hath forgiven you. (Ephesians 4:26; 4:32 KJV)

The Pain I Feel

There is a pain,
A pain too deep to pluck,
A pain too strong to dissolve,
A pain too much to define,
This is the pain,
The pain that I feel,

A pain too low to be lifted,
A pain too heavy to be carried,
A pain too hard to believe,
A pain too complex to imagine,
This is the pain,
The pain that I feel,

A pain too far to be seen,
A pain too small to touch,
A pain too big to handle,
A pain too good to be true,
This is the pain,
The pain that I feel,

A pain sharper than any sword,
A pain bitter than any pill,
A pain hotter than any furnace,
A pain stronger than any force,
This is the pain,
The pain that I feel,

Scripture: Let not your heart be troubled: ye believe in God, believe also in me. (John 14:1 KJV)

Is This Your Will?

Oh Lord my God,
Do you have to break me?
Each time that you make me,
Unto you I lift my face,
Show me your way, your truth

I thank you for the sound mind,
I meditate and think about your word,
Yet I do make wrong decisions,
With that same mind, Lord

I thank you for the friends you gave me,
Some truly inspire and urge me to go on,
Others however, turn to stab my back,
But you'd blessed me with them,

I thank you for all the teachers,
They taught me essentials about life,
Yet teachings are but for a season,
Father, do I really ever stop learning?

I thank you for this world, you created
I'm forever amazed by your handwork,
But evil does dwell in this world, too
Oh Lord my God, Is all this your will?

Scripture

Then said his wife unto him, Dost thou still retain thine integrity? Curse God, and die. But he said unto her, Thou speakest as one of the foolish women speaketh. What? Shall we receive good at the hand of God, and shall we not receive evil? In all this did not Job sin with his lips. (Job 2:9-10 KJV)

When thou passest through the waters, I [will be] with thee; and through the rivers, they shall not overflow thee: when thou walkest through the fire, thou shalt not be burned; neither shall the flame kindle upon thee. (Isaiah 43:2 KJV)

For You I Will

Indeed, I am determined
To block the sword
With my bare hands
Quench the fire with my breath
To swim right across the oceans
And jump off the mountains
Flying up high to catch a star
A lone battle, let it be
Even against a million men
In this narrow road
I shall squeeze myself through
Resisting every temptation
Drifting further away
From the crowd in the wide road
I shall rebuke them all
The principalities of darkness
Fighting a spiritual war
Against the lord of darkness
I shall persevere through it all
Even if it means
Going all way by myself
I shall rename loneliness to freedom
And keep His commandments at heart
Verily, He is within me
Therefore, I am not alone
I shall be steadfast in prayer
And give to Caesar
Only what belongs Caesar
Praising only Him
The one who is glorious

Hoping and trusting
That which I know
Knowing exactly what I believe
Believing in that which I hope
The hope brought forth with faith
Faith sustained by the works
Works which came from the word
The word which was there
From the beginning
In the beginning when God
Made a creation
Everything according to His will
His will and His purpose
His purpose with plans
Plans for me to prosper
All destined for me
Well before I was in the womb
That's why I live for Him
For you I will, Lord

Scripture

But we have this treasure in earthen vessels, that the excellency of the power may be of God, and not of us.
(2 Corinthians 4:7 KJV)

Before I formed thee in the belly I knew thee; and before thou camest forth out of the womb I sanctified thee, and I ordained thee a prophet unto the nations. (Jeremiah 1:5 KJV)

Poverty

Poverty, Poverty, Poverty
Struggling to meet
The demands of each day
Born like that
And even till death do you part!
A life in the negative
Paying old debts with new debts
Only have a better life
When lucky to dream of it!
Your friends and colleagues
All from the same class
All your blessings
Seem to turn into curses
You wonder why
But who can tell you why?

Hoping for the better
Is your talk everyday
When you were young
Your grandmother told you so
Now that you are old
You also tell your grand children
And your grand children
Will pass on the sermon
Down to the next blood line
Until a lucky generation
Finally receives that hope
The hope you have asked for
Prayed for and even waited for
And you wonder how

But who can tell you how?

Every broken piece
Never fit back to its position
You do more than enough
But it is never enough
Making ends meet
Really seems to be impossible
You think you are right
But maybe only in your wrongness
Nothing makes you smile
Except breathing for free
And as the sun goes down
You only wish to wake up and breathe
Life seems to be unfair
But maybe that is fair
And once more you wonder
But who can tell you?

Scripture

Better [is] the poor that walketh in his uprightness, than [he that is] perverse [in his] ways, though he [be] rich.
(Proverbs 28: 6 KJV)

Remember, there is a season and a time to every purpose under the heaven. (Ecclesiastes 3: 1 NIV)

All Because of You

I'm let down
Because of you men,
Because of you
Why do you fail to be grateful?
The birds in the sky,
Soaring and flying up high
Singing joyously
In mid-air with gratitude,
For all the food they get
Without sowing,
But you men,
You are always worried!

I'm feeling low
Because of you men,
Because of you
Why do you fail to forgive?
The cattle in your kraal,
After grazing they're relaxing
The young ones and the old,
All had reached an agreement,
They had forgiven you men
For stealing their milk,
But you men,
You rather live with bitterness!

I'm disappointed
Because of you men,
Because of you
Why do you fail to be obedient?

The sheep in your paddock,
They obey and follow your lead
Doing everything in togetherness,
As the shepherd instructs,
And all in one accord
Showing gentleness and humbleness,
But you men,
You struggle to follow Christ!

I'm really sad
Because of you men,
Because of you
Why fail to carry each other's burdens?
That horse in your stable,
Even when he is exhausted,
Still you take him for a ride
Whenever you desire,
With all your weight on his back,
He still runs with you
But you men,
You say, NO, to other's burdens!

I'm now angry!
Because of you men,
Because of you
Why do you fail to keep a promise?
Look at the rooster in your yard,
As simple as he is
In all seasons and in all weather,
He keeps the covenant,
In hunger and in good times,
The rooster crows every hour,
But you men,

You simply break your promises!

Scripture

Behold, how good and how pleasant [it is] for brethren to dwell together in unity! (Psalm 133:1 KJV)

Finally, [be ye] all of one mind, having compassion one of another, love as brethren, [be] pitiful, [be] courteous: Not rendering evil for evil, or railing for railing: but contrariwise blessing; knowing that ye are thereunto called, that ye should inherit a blessing. (1 Peter 3: 8- 9 KJV)

A Friend Indeed

A friend in need, you are my friend indeed,
An unconditional relationship, stronger than blood,
A genuine devotion with no harmful intention,
After all has been said and done,
Are you a friend indeed, my friend?

Altogether, we feasted on the same table,
An honourable master sat and ate with us,
Abundant blessings poured down on us,
Again and again, out of His tender mercies
Across all nations and tribes, it was witnessed

All which was yours, my friend, was mine
And that which was mine, also was yours
Amongst us, was oneness and faithfulness
As we were taught by our Master,
About loving one another, as you need to be loved

A word came as a prophecy, that day as we ate,
A betrayal was at hand, this supper was the last,
An act of rebellion, was with one of us,
An evil mind was to cost the life of our master,
And according to the word, the prophecy was fulfilled.

Scripture

Do not set foot on the path of the wicked or walk in the way of evil man. Avoid it and do not travel on it.
(Proverbs 4:14 – 15 NIV)

And forthwith he came to Jesus, and said, Hail, master; and kissed him. And Jesus said unto him, Friend, wherefore art thou come? Then came they, and laid hands on Jesus, and took him. (Mathew 26: 49 – 50 KJV)

Iscariot

From ear to ear,
You flashed a smile,
But the heart boiling with envy,
Iscariot!
Stop your fake smile,
Judgment day is coming,
Your true colours will be exposed

From morning to evening,
Promises are made,
But the heart telling lies,
Iscariot!
Stop your false promises,
The Heaven is watching you,
No lie shall inherit the Kingdom of God,

From left to right,
You embrace in hugs,
But the heart embracing bitterness,
Iscariot!
I need your hug no more,
The Lord is never mocked,
He shall bring you down to shame,

From your lips to my face,
You kissed me,
But the heart full of betrayal,
Iscariot!
You took your Master's life for granted,
But righteousness will ever prevail,

You shall take away your own life!

Scripture

A [good] name [is] rather to be chosen than great riches, [and] loving favour rather than silver and gold. (Proverbs 22:1 KJV)

Therefore the ungodly shall not stand in the judgment, nor sinners in the congregation of the righteous. For the LORD knoweth the way of the righteous: but the way of the ungodly shall perish. (Psalm 1:5-6 KJV)

Theorem of Vanity

Excuse me,
Mr. Ecclesiastes,
Do not be exclaimed, Sir
I am your student,
Please allow me over,
Did you really mean
What you preached?
About the vanity of vanities,
That all is vanity,
I had given a thought
About what you taught us,
That what goes around,
Always come back around?
True, there is no point in everything,
It is just meaningless,

Probably, you got
The benefit of my doubt,
To an extent we do share
The same school of thought,
For I humanly do not understand,
Why the sun set
When it shall rise again!
Why the sea is never full
Yet streams flow every day!
Why the eye is not satisfied
With seeing nor the ear
Filled up with hearing,
And why the rich man
Never takes his riches

To the grave!

Did you say there is a time,
For everything and every activity?
A time that can be there…
Anytime,
That gives a reason
Even for an unreasonable reason,
A time that cannot be…
Sometimes,
That makes sorrow
Be better than laughter,
A time that is available…
Every time,
That makes the end
Better than the beginning
Indeed, I salute you,
For the 'meaningless' teaching;

Scripture

Let us hear the conclusion of the whole matter: Fear God, and keep his commandments: for this [is] the whole [duty] of man. For God shall bring every work into judgment, with every secret thing, whether [it be] good, or whether [it be] evil. (Ecclesiastes 12: 13-14 KJV)

The Thief

STOLEN…
Reported the daily newspaper,
How possible, I thought
Alarm systems and security guards,
All in place,
How come then,
The perpetrator was too good?
We all know there are thieves and robbers, Fact.
But we all had failed to stop them,
Ready or not, here they come!
I can't see my wallet…
It's stolen

KILLED…
Reported the weekly press,
Who did it? I wondered
On this earth where we are
Supposed to live in harmony,
Why then, are there murders amongst us?
We all know that they do live, Fact.
But we all had failed to stop them,
Ready or not, here they come!
Gunshot…
One more is gone

DESTROYED…
Reported the monthly magazine,
Where exactly? I asked
With all these sophisticated detecting devices,
How then, do all these tragic happen?

We all know that disaster is there, Fact.
But we all had failed to stop it,
Ready or not, here it comes!
Boom…
Another city is bombed

Scripture

The thief cometh not, but for to steal, and to kill, and to destroy: I am come that they might have life, and that they might have [it] more abundantly. (John 10: 10 KJV)

Lost Souls

Like a most lost ghost,
You are hovering
Forever in darkness,
Wickedness is your middle name,
Doing good is definitely
Not found,
Even in your dreams,
You delight in evil,
You have no light!

Like a most lost ghost,
You are wondering
Forever in the midst of nowhere,
Lost for good,
Yet you hate to be directed,
Reaching destiny is
Not even in your dreams,
Your path is wrong,
You have no guidance!

Like a most lost ghost,
You are focusing
Forever at the present,
Your future is bleak,
Yet you hate to mould it,
The hope of tomorrow is
Not even in your dreams,
You are busy stagnating,
You have no progression!

Like a most lost ghost,
You are sleeping
Forever in your grave,
Resurrection is a promise,
Yet you hate to believe,
Life after death is
Not even in your dreams,
In you, there is no Christ,
You have no life!

Scripture

Blessed are they whose transgressions are forgiven, whose sins are covered. Blessed is the man whose sin the Lord will never count against him (Romans 4:7 – 8 NIV)

How think ye? if a man have an hundred sheep, and one of them be gone astray, doth he not leave the ninety and nine, and goeth into the mountains, and seeketh that which is gone astray? (Mathew 18: 12 KJV)

A Little Bit

Just a little bit,
Come and dance to this beat,
Everyone is on the rampage,
You got to be on the same page,
Come on and be in the midst,
Else you'll be lost in the mist,

There she is,
Kissing another girl,
She says that,
She feels like an angel,
He is here bragging,
He is in love with another man,
He says that,
He feels like a superhuman,
Hurry up now, they say
And join this fun,
Nobody shall give it a ban,
Do not let this chance,
Die alone on the floor,
Pick him up and flow,

There is so much fun
In this world,
You can't say this is weird,
Just a little bit,
Dance to this beat!

Scripture

*Now the works of the flesh are manifest, which are [these];
Adultery, fornication, uncleanness, lasciviousness, Idolatry,
witchcraft, hatred, variance, emulations, wrath, strife, seditions,
heresies, Envyings, murders, drunkenness, revellings, and such
like: of the which I tell you before, as I have also told [you] in time
past, that they which do such things shall not inherit the
kingdom of God. (Galatians 5:19-21 KJV)*

*And be not conformed to this world: but be ye transformed by the
renewing of your mind, that ye may prove what [is] that good,
and acceptable, and perfect, will of God. (Romans 12:2 KJV)*

*In a similar way, Sodom and Gomorrah and the surrounding
towns gave themselves up to sexual immorality and perversion.
They serve as an example of those who suffer the punishment of
eternal fire. (Jude 1: 7 NIV)*

Devil is a Liar

Devil you're a liar,
My Lord is a Messiah,
My deepest desire,
Is to see you in fire,
Furthermore, I shall require
To grip your demons with a wire,
I believe I've got that power,
And the whole world I'll inspire,
To take back what you'd acquire,
On that day in that hour,
Without this, I won't retire
Oh yes, I won't get tired,
I shall lift my head up higher,
To my God, I will enquire
His strength shall be my tower,
I will put on the whole armour,
When you come I shall hammer,
My faith is like of Hannah,
She received a child with honour,
My blessings shall drop like manna.

Scripture: Beware of false prophets, which come to you in sheep's clothing, but inwardly they are ravening wolves. Ye shall know them by their fruits. Do men gather grapes of thorns, or figs of thistles? (Matthew 7:15-16 KJV)

Finally, my brethren, be strong in the Lord, and in the power of his might. Put on the whole armour of God, that ye may be able to stand against the wiles of the devil. (Ephesians 6:10-11 KJV)

Fight A Good Fight

Congratulations,
You have made it,
A good fight, you had fought
Your effort had finally
Yielded some good fruits,
Indeed, your faith is not dead
Your works are here
For us to see,
The trials and temptations,
Came your way,
With prayer and supplication,
You pressed on,
Enduring longsuffering,
As the Apostles,
Who went before you,
With a humble heart,
Peace, love and joy,
You dwelt with,
The light of hope
Flickered ahead of you,
The wicked came,
With snares in your path,
But you never lost your track,
Even a cloud of darkness,
Was once over you,
But the light of God,
Was forever shining upon you,
Perseverance had made you,
To be more than a conqueror,
The Heaven is smiling,

The angels had kept you well,
For the purpose of God,
On earth you fulfilled,
As the whole duty of man,
You'd kept all His commandments,
A golden crown on your head,
For the job well done,
A good and faithful servant;

Scripture

Let us purify ourselves from everything that contaminates body and spirit, perfecting holiness out of reverence for God. (2 Corinthians 7: 1 NIV).

Be on your guard, stand firm in the faith; be men of courage, be strong. (1 Corinthians 16: 13 NIV).

Finally, my brethren, be strong in the Lord, and in the power of his might. Put on the whole armour of God, that ye may be able to stand against the wiles of the devil. (Ephesians 6: 10 – 11 KJV)

The Walk of Life

This day,
Absolutely no clue,
Of what tomorrow is to offer,
The certainty is very unpredictable,
To be on going
Or to be on a halt,
Progressing is entirely
On a hope,
Just like a bicycle tyre,

This day,
You aren't smiling at all,
Nothing is materialising,
It is going up the hill,
You really need to give it,
That extra strength,
Else, you will get nowhere
Or you will be taken aback,
Just like a bicycle tyre,

This day,
You feel great,
Things are just happening for you,
It is going downhill,
No much effort
Is being needed here,
Slow but sure,
You know you are getting there,
Just like a bicycle tyre,

This day,
You are indeed coping very well,
No hassling!
It is fairly a level ground,
You give it a push,
It moves away from you,
You pull it back,
It comes back to you,
Just like a bicycle tyre,

This day,
You are sobbing,
Actually down and out,
It is a puncture,
You won't get there,
Though you are trying hard,
Corrective measures are needed
For rectification,
Just like a bicycle tyre,

Scripture

See to it, brothers, that none of you has a sinful, unbelieving heart that turns away from the living God. But encourage one another daily, as long as it is called today, so that none of you may be hardened by sin's deceitfulness. (Hebrews 3: 12 – 13 NIV)

And we know that all things work together for good to them that love God, to them who are the called according to [his] purpose. (Romans 8: 28 KJV)

Nomutsa Oliver Madamombe

Die unto The Lord

Like a sudden change,
In the weather pattern,
An immediate swing of the wind,
With no appeal to rewind,
An abrupt ending to a road,
With no hope to reverse,
A sad loss of a memory verse,
The mind running wild,
In a bid to give a chase,
A rose blossoming in my face,
Now dying out leaving no trace,
The beautiful attraction once was,
Now turned to the worse,
Admirer's appetite left in a mess,
Like a race without a prize,
A good life with no future,
An amazing story with no meaning,
A fairy tale with no happy ending,
Like a puzzle with no solution,
The verdict of a powerful judge,
With no appeal for a resolution,
A sheep being led to the slaughter,
My cry is unheard of,
My plea is meaningless,
Even my life is worthless,
My happiness is ending today,
Slowly but surely it's happening,
Slowly but surely I'm being slain,
Slowly but surely, I'm dying,
Slowly but surely I'll be buried,

But a hope to resurrect lingers on,
I'm grateful I'm His son!

Scripture

What shall we then say to these things? If God [be] for us, who [can be] against us? Who shall separate us from the love of Christ? [shall] tribulation, or distress, or persecution, or famine, or nakedness, or peril, or sword? (Romans 8:31;35 KJV)

Blessed are ye, when [men] shall revile you, and persecute [you], and shall say all manner of evil against you falsely, for my sake. Rejoice, and be exceeding glad: for great [is] your reward in heaven: for so persecuted they the prophets which were before you. (Matthew 5:11-12 KJV)

For whether we live, we live unto the Lord; and whether we die, we die unto the Lord: whether we live therefore, or die, we are the Lord's. (Romans 14:8 KJV)

Never Lose Hope

I've got a non-stop terrible cough,
My days are becoming tough,
And the road I am is getting rough,

I've given all my best,
But things are getting worse,
My whole life is now a mess,
I truly need God's mercy,

I've got no money, no friends
Even my wife had abandoned me,
I thought we had vowed till death,
Only to realise I was wrong,

I'm actually fed up, much annoyed
With people always asking me, why?
Sometimes I wish that I could just die,
And be taken to a place which is most high,

But I won't stop to pray every hour,
For my healing to come sooner,
I believe everything is possible,
With the Holy Ghost power,

Scripture

In my distress I cried unto the LORD, and he heard me. Deliver my soul, O LORD, from lying lips, [and] from a deceitful tongue. (Psalms 120: 1- 2 KJV)

How Dare You, Death!

How dare you, death!
Always come to rob us
Of our beloved ones
At a time, we least expect a tragic
Who are you really?
A merciless creature
With no single feeling at all
How dare you…

Tell me,
Who shall provide for the orphans?
Tell me,
Who shall cater for the widows?
Tell me,
Why you took all those family members at once?
Tell me,
Why you want to keep that couple childless?
How dare you…

The accidents!
The car, bus and the plane crushes
Taking away millions of innocent souls
Twenty-four seven, 365 days
No off day nor leave!
Please take a breather now
Or better off, resign
How dare you…

Why do you marvel when people mourn?
Why do you hate to see the living?

Why did you take my brother, anyway?
At the moment we all thought he had recovered!
How dare you…

My desire is to see you dead one day!
So that you get the taste of your own medicine,
I know and believe, my desire shall come to pass
As the son of man had risen, so shall all the dead in Him,
How dare you, death!

Scripture

I am the resurrection and the life. He who believes in me will live, even though he dies; and whoever lives and believes in me will never die. Do you believe this? (John 11: 25 – 26 NIV)

For since death came through a man, the resurrection of the dead comes also through a man. (1 Corinthians 15: 21 – 22 NIV)

For ye are dead, and your life is hid with Christ in God. When Christ, [who is] our life, shall appear, then shall ye also appear with him in glory. (Colossians 3: 3 – 4 KJV)

The last enemy [that] shall be destroyed [is] death.
(1 Corinthians 15: 26 KJV)

What More Do You Want?

Finally, my brethren
What excuse will you give?
You of little faith
For how long
Will you remain unchanged?
Man of no hope
For how long
Will you remain doubtful?
The blind had received sight
In your presence
The sick was healed among you
The dumb spoke
And you talked with them
The deaf heard your praises
As you exclaimed with joy
The lame got up on their feet
And together you walked back home
The crippled were made perfect
Right before your eyes
The Holy Spirit himself
Had manifested in you
You spoke in tongues,
You saw the visions,
You began to prophecy,
You were given dreams,
You casted out demons,
And you even healed the sick,

Your sins were washed away
By the precious blood

The blood of a begotten son
JESUS CHRIST
Who humbled himself
Up to the cross
The cross he passionately carried
With our burdens
Burdens which had alienated us
Away from His presence

My brethren
Will you choose to die?
Because of lack of knowledge?
You of little faith
What more do you want?
For you to believe
Man of no hope,
Where do you think
This world came from?

Scripture

And without faith it is impossible to please God, because anyone who comes to him must believe that he exists and that he rewards those who earnestly seek him. (Hebrews 11: 6 NIV)

I have spoken to you of earthly things and you do not believe; how then will you believe if I speak of heavenly things. (John 3: 12 NIV)

Jesus answered them, I told you, and ye believed not: the works that I do in my Father's name, they bear witness of me. But ye believe not, because ye are not of my sheep, as I said unto you. (John 10: 25 – 26 KJV)

Winning Souls

'Brilliant Gooooaaaal!'
Exclaimed the commentator,
The dribbling striker,
Had proved his mettle,
Sending the goalie in the opposite direction,
A wave of cheer,
Suddenly appears in the crowd,
The prestigious cup is won,
Courtesy of the goal,

'Howz-iiiiiiiiiiiiiiiiit!!'
Shouted the bowler and his mates,
The left hand spinner,
Deceived the batsman nicely,
Forcing him to put his leg before wicket,
Everybody shouts as the umpire raises his finger,
All wickets are gone;
The test match is won,

'Deuce,'
Calmly said the umpire,
From side to side,
The ball got hit continuously,
'Advantage,' the ball finally rests into the net
Again, another series of hits,
But not so long,
'Match point,' everybody claps,
The game is over,

'Repent now!'

Said the preacher man,
From Genesis to Revelations,
The scriptures are read,
Urging all non-believers,
To give their life to Jesus,
All the angels in Heaven look down on earth,
Suddenly, great joy fills Heaven;
The lost soul is won,

Scripture

I say unto you, that likewise joy shall be in heaven over one sinner that repenteth, more than over ninety and nine just persons, which need no repentance. It was meet that we should make merry, and be glad: for this thy brother was dead, and is alive again; and was lost, and is found. (Luke 15:7;32 KJV)

For my Father's will is that everyone who looks to the Son and believes in him shall have eternal life, and I will raise him up at the last day. (John 6: 40 NIV)

God Bless Africa

She carries a heavy load,
She suffers rejection,
She endures isolation,
She feels all the tension,
She longs for protection,

She carries a heavy burden,
Her people are exploited,
Her resources are exploited,
Her land is also exploited,
She longs to be respected,

She carries a heavy load,
She's senselessly attacked,
She's scornfully mocked,
She's sourly grieved,
She longs to be comforted,

She carries a heavy burden,
Consider her ways, oh Lord,
Heal her land for she's humble,
Forgive and redeem her, oh Lord,
She longs to be blessed,

Scripture

If my people, which are called by my name, shall humble themselves, and pray, and seek my face, and turn from their wicked ways; then will I hear from heaven, and will forgive their sin, and will heal their land. (2 Chronicles 7:14 KJV)

The End of Times

Like an old piece of rag,
You tore my motherland into tatters,
The original home of mankind,
Where missionaries flocked into,
From yester years,
A paradise on earth, it was
Full of splendour, minerals and peace
The man and the animals,
All dwelt in harmony,
But now…
It's another page of history,
Where have you gone to,
Days of the past?
Shall we say you were better
Than this day?
Hunger is holding us,
By our throats,
Starvation is gripping our midst,
War and fighting is unending,
Incurable diseases are vast,
Wiping us off the earth,
The love of money is on the lips,
Loving one another,
Is just but a secondary issue,
Sexual immorality now a hobby,
Jealous and selfishness,
Flying everywhere, as if normal
Corruption has ruined the economy,
The glamour and the splendour
Had vanished since long,

How can we not say?
This is the end of times,
Are these signs not evident?

Scripture

And Enoch also, the seventh from Adam, prophesied of these, saying, Behold, the Lord cometh with ten thousands of his saints, To execute judgment upon all, and to convince all that are ungodly among them of all their ungodly deeds which they have ungodly committed, and of all their hard [speeches] which ungodly sinners have spoken against him. (Jude 1: 14 -15 KJV)

In the last times there will be scoffers who will follow their own ungodly desires. These are the men who will destroy you, who follow mere natural instincts and do not have the spirit. (Jude 1:17 – 19 NIV)

Here I Come, Lord

On my knees I fall,
In Jesus' name I call,
In your presence I bow,
My redeemer is none but you,
You delivered me from shame,
You cleansed me from blame,
By your Holy name,
I'll forever bless you,
With all that is within me,
Unto you Lord I come,
A new creation I'd become,
Renew in me a right Spirit,
And let your Holy Spirit,
Give me words of prayer,
Yes, set me on fire,
Fire for the Messiah,
To burn all evil,
Ignite my inner man,
My life is not mine,
My life is yours,
Unto you I come,
I surrender all,
Here I am to worship,
As the deer thirsts for water,
My soul longs for you,
As a living vessel,
I'll live for you

Scripture

Draw nigh to God, and he will draw nigh to you. Cleanse [your] hands, [ye] sinners; and purify [your] hearts, [ye] double minded. (James 4:8 KJV)

Come unto me, all ye that labour and are heavy laden, and I will give you rest. (Mathew 11:28 KJV)

Perfect Place

There is a place,
A place that awaits me,
Glory shall run down my face,
My face which had ran tears,
No more sorrow shall I face,
In this perfect place,
My dwelling there is by grace,
The grace I received at no price,
From the nailing of Him on the cross,
By those who showed Him no mercy,
But He will forever show goodness,
In this perfect place,
Shall reign all the saints,
Called out from the book of names,
True is every verse,
Praise Him, King of kings,
Every tongue shall confess,
In this perfect place,
This is a promise,
That I heard from His voice,
That's how my soul rejoice,
Indeed, I shall rise,
Soaring on eagle's wings,
Into this perfect place,

Scripture

But they that wait upon the LORD shall renew [their] strength; they shall mount up with wings as eagles; they shall run, and not be weary; [and] they shall walk, and not faint. (Isaiah 40:31 KJV)

In my Father's house are many mansions: if [it were] not [so], I would have told you. I go to prepare a place for you. And if I go and prepare a place for you, I will come again, and receive you unto myself; that where I am, [there] ye may be also. (John 14:2-3 KJV)

Joy in Heaven

Sing Hosanna,
Hallelujah, Sing Hosanna,
It's a huge noise,
Unheard of on earth,
A very loud noise
But never annoys,
It's a rejoice,
Made of singing in joy,
As all saints gather,
To meet the Almighty Father,
At His throne,
Everyone is getting a crown,
At His throne,
Ever glory is thrown,
In this Heaven,
There is no single heathen,
All the praises,
Is from the chosen among races,
It's a blessed Kingdom
Unlike the cursed Sodom,
All shout 'Holy'
To worship Him only,
Every spiritual hymn,
Is sung unto Him,
On the right hand is Jesus,
Who had redeemed us,
With Him is Lord,
The Heavenly God,
Sin in Heaven
Is truly unseen,

There is no disease;
The health is at ease,
No division and fights,
But divine rights,
There is no death,
Because every saint is worthy,
Absolutely no evil,
For there is no devil,
And all angels praise,
Bowing from all angles,
My brethren,
Do well now,
So that you dwell there!

Scripture

But lay up for yourselves treasures in heaven, where neither moth nor rust doth corrupt, and where thieves do not break through nor steal. (Mathew 6: 20 KJV)

So with you: Now is the time of grief, but I will see you again and you will rejoice, and no one will take away your joy. (John 16: 22 NIV)

Unfulfilled Love Story

You needed it
Aimed to reach but cannot hold it
Fingers have been stung
So bad so much they hurt
A bitterness in the back of mind
Wondering what could have been
A loss of hope, a life lost
A disfigured focus

Forgive and forget
You practiced and moved on
But feelings have been stung
So bad so much they hurt
Roots run so deep
Memories just cannot fade away
A loss of trust, a love lost
An unfaithful partner

Try to recuperate
Do not lose the faith, they said
But you've been stung
So bad so much the swelling is intense
The odds have been stacked
All but against you, it seemed
A loss of sight, a vision lost
A mission unaccomplished

The whole body aches
Even little children know
You've been stung so bad

So much your senses malfunctioned
Cannot trust anybody any more
The odds cannot balance, it seemed
A loss of heart, a feeling lost
An unfulfilled love story

* This poem is extract from upcoming book:
- Teenage Love Syndrome -

Paradise of Love

Take me to paradise
Before I die
Show me the intrinsic
That I knew not
The eerie and unknown path
Of a rocky surface
The formula that yields
The much awaited revelation
Give me the keys
To thy holy of holies
Carve in me
An unforgettable sculpture

That can only resonate
For decades to come
A once upon a time
Sacred intimacy
That stands right now,
Straight in my face
Let me feel that feeling
I had never felt before
Let them pour out profusely
The tears of joy
Let me forget
Even my very own name

Engrave love in my memory
A lasting impression
Which shall never end,
Let it run up to infinity
And there shall we stay

Forever in our fairy tale
For that ending is
Nothing short of only happiness
Now bring me closer
And hold me tighter
Let me just die now
In this paradise of love

* This poem is extract from upcoming book:
- Teenage Love Syndrome -

To God be all the glory.

The end

www.ingramcontent.com/pod-product-compliance
Lightning Source LLC
LaVergne TN
LVHW011213080426
835508LV00007B/765